COMES A TIME OF NO RETURN

J.T. DODDS

Cover Photo: Pexels-Wendel Moretti

77 Rio Papaloapan
Ajijic, Jalisco, México 45920
Tel: 376 766 3327
Cell: 52 332 605 5432
jtdodds@hotmail.com

DEDICATION

To Candis, the inspiration for my humble attempts at
viewing the possibilities of a better world

CONTENTS

PROSE

Also by John Thomas Dodds

Poetry

In Our Own Backyard
A Still Silent Space
Sen-Essence
Aging Beautifully in Light of You
A Stroll Through the Village of Ajijic
Small Altars Where the Sun Performs
Places That Hold An Energy Of Love
Footprints In The Dust
Learning To Lean Back On Living
Kats Kids & Kreativity
Father Hunting
Free To Be Me
Gone Fishing

Children's Poetry

A Sneaky Twitch of an Itch
A Journey Home

Fiction

Anywhere Except Yesterday (J.T. Dodds)
A Long Way From Nowhere (J.T. Dodds)
When Somewhere Is Never enough (J.T. Dodds)
If You Are Born to be a Tamale(J.T. Dodds)
Wanting To Breathe Her In (J.T. Dodds)

At first we danced the mazurka

In the end, everyone is aware of this:
nobody keeps any of what they have,
and life is only a borrowing of bones.

y a fin de cuentas ya lo saben todos:
nadie se lleva nada de su haber
y la vida fue un préstamo de huesos.
-Pablo Neruda

Comes a Time of No Return

A coming of age moves you from the center of the universe to an ever expanding understanding of just where you might fit in—assuming of course you listen.

Some, like the snowdrops, enter in act one, acknowledge an audience, and disappear.

Others, like the Hawthorne tree, wait until everything around them blends to the moment, and guarding against trespass are last to leaf and first to leave.

Aging allows you to render the bark around you as part of yourself. Even in the shedding of mindfulness, greycells synapse into the ozone, everything that means something closes in, becomes important, if only to you, and to what you are, to what you love, and who loves you.

Some enter screaming onto a tapestry of color that never dulls from the wear, and washing of lifetimes.

Others slip silently into a white antiseptic wrap, their story never heard.

If you have managed to leave alone everything that has touched you, aging is the glue that sticks the pictures to the pages of memories that mean the most. Memories you cannot delete, re-minding you of why you are here, not just still here, here in the hearts of everyone that has orbited around your star.

Some age slowly, others blossom and are gone.
Some stick like mud and harden in the sunlight.
Others are a wisp of dust in a breeze.

When you reach a point in the long deep obsidian season of the mind, waiting to feel the reflection of your story, there appears out of nowhere a covey of snowdrops huddled together in a garden of dirt brown leaves and winter wreckage. A point in time where, rather than from the internal combustion of a dark and dis-tempered soul, in the comfort of an all-encompassing light there appears a promissory note in the greeting of dawn.

Not just another day aging along, stumbling upon potential fulfillment, just possibly coming to terms with the aging process we never leave behind or plan for.

Comes an age where we are thankful for the oneness of the day. Comes an age asking only to be helpful, to be of service.

There's a Seasonal Thing

There's a seasonal aspect to this life we live,
benchmarks that have a history, quarterly
objectives unmet and mastered, mile markers
you remember passing along the way.

Good feelings ingrain themselves
at a very early age and never let go, Only,
if only you enter laughing and somehow
never let go of the possibilities,
no matter how slight the meaning of joy,
        for misery needs a definition
        and wanting comes with loss.

There are blocks of life where life has left
holes in the garment I was born to wear.
Years where the waves came crashing in,
where the sands tumbled into empty spaces
leaving gold nuggets and empty shells.
Times sucked into the undertow
of subliminal anxiety and fear of knowing,
into the comfort of silence and forgetfulness.

Nothing to hide, nothing to remember.
The broom and dustpan of our memory
sweeping anything and everything into
the holes we create in our conscience.
Where all, all thoughts and actions,
from the sublime to the inhumane,
        can be forgiven.

The Pendulum Swings

the pendulum swings
for that is what it is
and with it,
ups and downs
that never end,

Poe knew,
and so to,
every dreamer and schemer
that ever put pen to paper

comes a time
to fine tune
when the fork will slow
to the vibration of a single note,

what the Poet wrote
when penning
the universal scheme

in balance,
the in-between
in this lifetime
the experience
is the dream

Do It When You Think of It

Do it when you think of it
or it will slip your mind,
     you will leave forever
     the thought behind.

For everything is happening
at once: everything that can be,
     everything that will be,
     and all the in-between.

We are no Different you and I.
No different than the sea to sky,
     we laugh, we play,
     we cry, we pray.

We colorfast the world around us
share the day and share the night,
it is perchance how you and I relate.
     we learn to love,
     we learn to hate,

The wonderful thought of how
a world should be in the instant
before memory, is the essence
     of everything that is.

If it is Not Exactly

If it is not exactly
as you would like it,
well maybe, not even close,
it's all that you have
in the present moment,
do nothing for it takes
but a mindset
to turn it around.

You are here,
you are breathing,
vertical to the ground.
.The cat meows
like a banshee
keeping you awake.
Take a deep breath,
and be grateful
you can hear the sound.

You bought into
the darkness.
The sun doesn't shine.
Anger and distrust
is your frame of mind.
If it is not exactly
as you would like it,
Time to turn it around.

Life Comes at You Like a Freight Train

Life comes at you
like a freight train
rattling your bones,
your shadow shudders
and your timber groans.

vacant sighs haunt the lives
of souls left living,
sound stills the space
between pauses
in a momentary freezing
of the frames that qualify
and quantify a life

the trees, barely naked,
cold cleans the air
leaving nothing
but a pale blue sky,
overnight memories
disappear in thin air
all that survives
are the remains

lives here are mostly
skin and bone
boredom breeds heroes
love is left alone

All We Have Known and Cared For

We squirrel away pieces of friends,
family, and ourselves in our need
to gather to hold on as if forever.
Somehow they get buried in time.

What do we really keep of one another?

Souvenirs of occasion,
        whatever's,
whatnots to remember us by,

pictures stuffed in shoe boxes,
casual acquaintances,
        quaint places,
        curious faces

So much of the stuff of loved ones

The mind has a wonderful way
of holding on to all that it encounters
on this shared journey we are on.

We need only to be the keepers
        of the world around us
        to love the memory
of all that we have known and cared for.

There's a Harry in All of Us

There's a Harry in all of us
        trying to be
what we think we ought to be.

Wanting to say
what we think we would say
if we could only go beyond craft
        and say it with talent.

Trying to rhyme,
            writing line after line,
scraping away at the surface of things—
every time coming out smiling
        like sweat wallowing
in the right life,   wrong timing.

No wonder afterlife is so compelling.

We live knowing we are not alone,
            thinking that we are,
and after all is said and done

believing we'll rest eternally with everyone.

Long Lineage Of Poet Saints

Coming from a long lineage
        of poet saints

The forgotten offspring of Mira
        the laughter of God
                the remnants of Rumi

it is not that I have heard
God whispering in my ear,

or felt the Spirit laying down
beside me in a lover's embrace

it is that I have penned already,
and forever to be repeated,
the sigh that comes from knowing
the beauty of a universal plan

should there be one

Some Days

Some days first snow intrudes,
    an omen of more to come.

Some days come and go,   when
you can't remember,   what

    shirt you wore yesterday
    you had for lunch
    you were supposed to
    pick up on the way home.

Some days are troublesome
    some trouble free

Some full of fend and forgive

    with a promise of a better day

joyful of remembering in kindness

    all that has passed away,

knowing in one's heart

    forever is but a day away.

The protagonist

Suppose you could craft your own tale,
not minding that you're on life's stage
a byproduct of a happenstance casting,
the expectation of a run, but a season.

Once penned and playable you're story
gets top billing, as long as it captivates,
keeping applause alive, reviews alluring.

How long will it take to realize nothing
really matters, except what lingers after
the house lights dim on an empty stage.

In the silence of passing comes the Call
for other characters; your posters, stored
in a hall of fame, open only on demand.

Soliloquy's fade, and any one star becomes
a glimpse among the minions of a dark sky.

The Outhouse

The outhouse solemnly squatting
in an insular field, a safe distance from
daily activities, is where it all begins.

Seated on a pedestal in deep thought,
Rodin's contemplative Poet am I,
exploring how life flows through me.

The remnants of which, unnecessary
and unfulfilled desires are safely rejected,
while contemplating time well spent.

Following a rewarding digestive, flush
with age, the slate clean, still leaves me
unfulfilled, sitting on remnants of dreams.

Having served a decomposing purpose,
soon to be extinct as the notable outhouse,
inevitably unseated by a porcelain throne.

In the end, motility slows to breaking wind,
leaving it all behind, is where it all ends,
eminently satisfying the phrase,
          you can't take it with you.

Expecting the Worst

Here's how you play the game of preparing for the worst of anything and everything.

Number of Players: There are no limits to the number of players. Group dynamics however will considerably extend the playing time with the introduction of blame, indecision and lack of introspection.

Rules of the Game: You are to look at all possible scenarios of the situations presented, real or imagined, and play out the self-imposed obstacle course on the road to achievement.

In Preparation: pretend you are a clairvoyant of occasions, never to miss anything that might happen, creating out of thought and speculation the "just in case" worst scenario possible.

Conjure up the negative side of what might happen and before you ever reach the point you are converging on, throw up as many new barriers, obstacles and seemingly irreversible possibilities as you can imagine.

Try to constantly control what might arise at any given moment, and if you don't think it will turn out as expected (know ing it won't turn out), step back, analyze potential for other than you thought it would be, prepare for the inevitable, whatever might be.

Plan: for unexpected and disastrous results, anticipating everything that will go wrong. Advance with trepidation and fear after each setback.

Hints: Look for things to go wrong. If you are stuck and can't find any, invent them.   If it doesn't happen exactly how you expected it to, it probably wasn't supposed to, so be prepared to accept the least. If you so badly want it to be other than it is or presumably will be—worry it to death.

How to Win the Game: You win, of course, when you are knee deep in shit and you turn it over to the Big Guy and say Show me the way.

Buggy Whip

I marvel at the speed
of daylight chasing shadows,
only to transition from
deification to mundanity,
and then I don't

I wonder at the assimilation
of once unimaginable
switches turning on
a revolving world,
and then I don't,
give it a second thought

it's called progress,
take it or leave it
as if it were a bar of soap
washing away the struggle
it took to turn on the light

necessity replicating
the wonder of mind
and body once called
garden of perfection,
then it doesn't

I'm guilty of taking
for granted the present,
as if yesterday never happened

On the cusp of three quarters

On the cusp of three quarters
and change, I'm on a brisk ride.

The battery still holds a charge,
the software, however, out dated.

The morning school bus turns
around on my dead end Calle,
ready to offload the next generation.

The rattle and hum of another year
is a cross between a chortle and
my two tom's stuck in a face off.

There's no return, or starting over.
What used to be a sweet download
buffers away forever and a day.

When the apple's ripe on the tree,
nothing remains but to savor to the core.

The Music You Love

The music you love no longer plays
at the top of the charts, the melody
that rattles in your morning mind is vinyl,
stages of your life begin and end
like mile markers on the interstate,
remembrance becomes a veteran's
parade of wars with the newest
and the oldest stepping in time.

Supposing there's a logical reason
you are known by what you did,
and where it all began, yet somehow
it chaffs of greatness bending to the whims
of what matters for what was left behind.

What remains after the flood, the drought,
the insanity of scorched earth and genocide
is the cream that always rises to the top,
and always will, a common lesson in gratitude
for the moment, and a promise of better things
to come, just because it makes sense.

Songs grow old and lose their shape,
memories linger long in the recesses of the mind.

Ever present, we wait for the future
to sit down beside us, and listen to the music.

Waltzing in and out of each year, always chasing rainbows in a whimsy fantasia.

Re-tire Re-tread Re- make

Time comes
when you need to stop expanding
in the universal scheme of things
whoadown, slow down,
leave behind the rebound,
spend time staying healthy
doing the daily comealong,
and not much more.

Re-mind ,re-start, re-take,
go with the flow
of a transcending theme

quantity dis-abled, quality en-abled,
joy embedded in the doing,
and so much more.

It's all about making room
for the new shoots,
nature nudging you to go out
and play, reinventing yourself
versus becoming a product
of a disposable world.

If you don't use it,
        you know,
it wears down from
lack of friction with life,
        and rusts.

Waking To Nobodies Home Anymore

Everybody knows about the hole in the bucket. It's where reality, as you think you know it, the visible world on the other side of the plate glass window of your mind, slowly leaks into the emptiness of time and space. Until one day you find you have arrived in the present, and the bucket's empty.

        You have entered the void.

How is it that the illusion of happiness, the lingering smell of sweat and damp sheets, the cocoon of comfort wrapped around the brain can, in the course of a conversation, over a cup of coffee or sitting on the edge of the bed, turn into an aloneness without substance, an accumulation of a lifetime of togetherness

        with nothing to hold onto.

Nothing tangible, nothing real remaining, except in the mind, where thoughts like shards of shattered mirror reflect the residue of breakfast Christmas mornings, pregnant days of mythical contentment and satisfaction. The aftermath of which the sun leaks through a shade-less window onto a mattress on the floor

        in an empty room,

The temptation is to fill the void with what the sentient
body craves: memories of touch, vibrant, smooth and
gentle, a breath of warmth, softly caressing what you
assumed possessed you. Waking to nobodies home
anymore means you are left to your own rewards.
There's a groove in the CD, right where the heartache
begins.
                    time to buy some new music.

          This time make it something you like.
               The sound of your voice
          in the morning affirming you are okay.

     Nothing real can happen until you are satisfied
               with the face in the mirror—
          with how you feel about yourself.

          It has never been complicated,
     if you can't cook, stay out of the kitchen.

               if you don't love yourself,
          leave romance well enough alone.

Thankful Frets

Stitches disappear
bulbous body parts
absolve, flatten,
fear resolves into memory
of what you thought
might happen

if only you had known
would you have done
anything different
or would you have just
lain there belly up
accepting what came your way,
accepting

in retrospect
healing never ends

anticipation of another
turn in the road
is understanding
the road forever bends
turn-about are never ending
and stopping now and then
is simply let's begin again

Nothing Changes, Yet...

Everything does
what it is supposed to do,
exchange a moment for a moment,
a time in line with itself
curving ever back upon itself
repeating that which is,
until all is visible, all is light.

The same songs are sung over and over again,
the same person walks in and out of your life,
the same painting hangs on the wall,
                              until you can see it

then it becomes as it always has,
an image that reappears
until awareness takes hold ,
and you see all of that which
is visible through an inner light.

If you are so inclined to repeat
that which you have already seen,
a reawakening of a previous dream,

it is telling you to look beyond the visible

and seek the changeless in-between

Bonematter

The journey has begun!
I feel it in my bones
osteoporosis and me,
no matter, no bonematter
it's maybe the heart of the matter

other organs dissolving,
tissue, cells and enzymes
not so subtly shifting
to another space and time

backspace, headspace,
elbows and toes
they all go, sooner,
hopefully later,
and how sweet it is

think of it as
the time required
for the flavor to set in
liken to the aging of the grape
potato salad savoring overnight
wine left open to breathe
only to be consumed with pleasure
once aged and agreed upon

this trip is kids' stuff
scrapes and bruises
stubs and stickers
compared to mingling
with the par-tic-ular universe
beyond the speed of sight and sound
hanging around in a void
of time and space

what makes this place
at times, seem tough to leave,
is rubbing up against
the experience of thought,
translated in the rough

as some thing or other to please,
and living on dying
while leaving a trace,
might just be a perceptual tease

God's Gift To Aging Bards

God's gift to aging poets
is convenient lapses of memory,
without which scraps of paper,
scribbles, and scratched out rhymes
would inundate the mind
leaving nothing behind.

If all the poets within you
      lined up on parade,
each would have book in hand
written in sand
for the waves of time to wash away.

Every poem ever written
      by a poet thus smitten,
takes a chance of being well-spoken
or never given   a second glance

      so for the poem
that is lost to the eye,
for the voice not yet heard
for those leafed in a book,
a letter bundled,
      in a stationary repose
      I suppose it is said,
laid to bed, to arise
when needing to be read

The Way Wood Weathers

There will come a time,
I know, from what I sense,
        a time of undoing itself

the way wood weathers while still
        clinging to the tree.

        there will come a time

the distance between moving towards,
and away from,
is all there will be to think of

when doors open
and necessity begs an audience,
when doing is an act
of forgiveness with gravity

        the body knows.
it slows,
if it survives long enough,

and settles
arthritically into the gap
between the tick   and the tock

Since We Talked Of Growing Old Together

I am slowly learning
to take a swift look at the past
& a sweet look at the future

when I hold autumn
against my senses

when the air hangs
with the aroma of fresh linen

when all the roses
are wearing raindrops

I don't suppose it matters
that it has only been forever

since we talked
of growing old together

Men as they age

Turn into cooks and cleaners
as if the less they have to do,
the more they are able to do,
in the art of living.

For some, the mechanics of it
gives way to the subtle blending
of ginger, curry, fresh cut vegetables,
sauteing in a pot thirsty for broth.

For others, living in a space
compatible with the essence
generated by a loving relationship,
is all about playing upon
the subtlety of the moment,
the aliveness of the moment,
just being in a dance together
simmering in a sensuous sauce.

Then again, not all men
intend upon the now and again,
sadly missing the point of being,
able to give, and let live,
                in the art of living.

Defying Gravity in a Hamaca

Certainly I'm not the only one
of sidereal significance
        fixed to a distant star,
feet firmly planted on a spinning teetotum
precariously balanced
        on the breaking point

gasping onto air,
knowing full well the unknown
        can bring out the eraser
        hit the delete button
reach the tipping point of no return,
        all in one revolution

With no breaks on the spin of things.
earth twirling like a column of Bobos
        I should be in a tailspin
instead of dancing with the swallows,
instead of slow dragging time.

Leaving gravity in a hammock,
is no longer an object in motion
no longer accelerating
        like a ripple of a wave
            on a pebbled shore
waiting for Newton's application
of an outside force to change direction

The clay of us has a tendency

The clay of us
has a tendency
to harden as it ages

Soft comes
with memories
out of reach,
touch becomes
an elixir for the soul.

In the crucible of time,
we mold our essence,
we are shaped
sculpted and draped
in the dance of joy
and the shadows of strife

In echoes of laughter,
we find a resilience,
a malleability of the mind

When tears have dried
a sigh settles
on our lap and purrs.

Survival

An essential purpose of life,
such as it is for many, survival,
strives to fill the belly of the soul,
while inherent disaster plays away
at chances of hope and possibilities
with each opportunity at the table.

Life on the promise of today,
with its deposits and withdrawals,
blank checks on an empty account,
tarnished silver spoons, yesterday's
leftovers of a bygone golden age,
are rent due valentine cards that
once held the promise of tomorrow

If you're the eight ball, and the game
is being human, it's all about
being the last one left standing
at the table you claim to be yours,
then you get to pocket the moment,
before the white one
          finds a hole to stuff you in.

Toward The Big Pond

Patience again sleeps restless
        at my door

One would think
        I would learn in time,

the faster I go

the slower I get

All the sentient and inert
  helter-skelter in the current,
        bubbling alone at warp speed

toward the big pond
  of empty expectations
        of everything I have asked for

the more I remember
        the more I forget

the less I remember
        the less I regret

Memory or No Memory

Just a question
on abdicating responsibility
in the land-of-forget-me-nots.

Where greycells become the dandruff
of should haves and oops,

maybe, if only, I had remembered
what I...

Everyone leaves his or her mind behind
when they climb the stairs
enter a room
go after something that,
just an interminable second ago,
was the most important priority,
focus, quest, on their agenda.

The mind sometimes,
is peculiar to itself,
and ignores your concern.

Nothing particular, has an age about it,
except what others perceive,
transform in their minds what is
in their consideration,
what old should look like.

Weathered being the primary observation
linked to previous exposure.

Nothing sticks
when whatever
the day brings
is just the way it is,

for the older you get,
the harder you get.

The more a word, an innuendo,
a tone taken tips the balance
of pain and pleasure.

the older you get,
the softer you get.

Memory or no memory,
just another way
of saying, been there,
done with that.

life becomes a polonaise,
a slow march on the ivories,

SomeTimes in Life

None of the pieces fit the puzzle
the only way out, the only respite
from insanity is a non-judgmental
absence from reality wrapping
unity in a tear while hope cowers
behind a wall of doubt, waiting
silently for a compassionate miracle,
       too often waiting for not.

Yesterday seems a long way away
from today, the melody stays
as if in a dream, nothing changes
nothing it appears remains the same
shadow & light garden in a never ending
moment of flight, searching for answers
that dissipate in a fog of disbelief
       & fading memory.

Going nowhere on a neglected highway,
way past the due date, waiting
for an auspicious moment to pass on bye
takes a toll, waiting while the morning rain
hangs on to the fleeting darkness
until yesterday crawls out of bed
slams the door shut without a goodbye.

Time Passengers

Being Human,my mortality express
is destined for the final stop.
        As far as tomorrow,
the no return ticket, will allow.

A free gift from a smiling task master
sitting on a cloud of possibility
handing out due dated itineraries
with blank arrivals and departures.

Means of travel varying depending
on the luck of my birthright;
first class, coach or baggage.

As a time passenger I'm
on a preordained journey
guided by circumstances
        beyond my control

arriving and leaving
stations along the stations,
inevitable milestones:
where songs everybody sang
trend into old adverts
and words seek clarity,
become malleable as if soft clay.

Time of destination
stamped by a conductor,
announcing the inescapable reality
the trip will be no longer
          than the time it takes
to say hello and goodbye.

Recall

If I could recall my every story ever lived it would always end right here. This October sky sun warmed and shimmering off the burnished silver waters of Narragansett Bay, Van Morrison wailing soulfully in the background, beside a loving presence shared in the romance and passion of the moment.

For some ungodly reason, we think we need to settle loose ends, recall everything, and everybody unfinished, fire and glaze what our hands have molded out of clay regardless of the quality and subject of the matter.

We've all collected bagfuls of stories without endings: *the wolf never showed up, the crows ate the bread crumbs, the shoe didn't fit, neither the prince nor princess woke up.*

We've all walked through a forest of paragraphs without beginnings or endings: *speaking for myself, of course, we've willingly taken to the depths the emotions of being there, in a process that necessarily leads to forgetfulness...*

We've all lived poems that dropped off the page: *you can forgive yourself for not finishing the story, sans denouement, he died of old age, unfinished…*

The temptation is to helix around another person's journey, the toil and trouble of which would shred the wings of butterflies, move you away from yourself, slip you out of your perfectly balanced orbit into the never ending narrative of someone else's story.

Not One to Borrow Trouble

Why is it when everything seems to be going
as planned, doubt slips in, and questions
flavored with fear, generate indecision.

The fog of differing self slips under the door,
envelopes a conflicted mind in dis-grace.
Thought's, trapped in perceived limitations
and insipid soul consuming worry, step up,
                  and you close down.

If sadness is to come of it,
since stories hidden and suppressed
unravel in the end, what is it that prevents
the telling of the truth, when the thought occurs.
The truth as one and all know it to be.

Not wanting to make waves,
upset the apple cart, cross any bridges
                  before you come to them,
trouble hides behind a smother of silent guilt,
where misplaced fears are buried, deep
within the mindful realm of the unforgiven.

Sonorous with age the soul sometimes
                    has need to vent.
Trouble borrowed or lent will,
on its' own, rise to the surface
where it takes as much consciousness
        to hold on to secrets,
as it does to let them go.

If you are not one to borrow trouble,
all but the sorrow will settle indiscreetly
in the deepest recesses of the heart.
The mind will hold onto the pain
ensuring itself a life of its own,
                and you go on living with
your dirty little surreptitious thought.

In the end, everything washes ashore,
worrisome wears thin with a waning spin
and guilt, burrowed and buried in shame,
rises to the surface.

Truth would have it, tells all in the end,
and barters not the emotions
                nor favors foe or friend.

Aging vacillates

Between acceptance and intolerance
or is it that we reach a stage of gestation
where we just don't care
to hold anything inside, anymore.

There's a stage of -agenarian
development where it's not worth
maintaining a decorum of politeness
when it comes to natural functions;
breathing, expressing an opinion,
            and of course flatulating.

Bodily functions have a humor
all their own: kids guffaw at farts,
women smile at fluffs, and old farts
            just don't give a damn.
Nobody talks about it.
Everyone turns their head and ignores it.
            Life goes on.

On any given day, everything consumed,
            is digested and then exuded.
It's how books are written and read.
It's how thoughts are shaped and spread,
how life absorbs creation and is put to bed.

Existence

No matter how long it takes
there is an ending
to everything.

Is it possible
that what we are after,
after all,
is an expression of self,

and in that,
an understanding
of what it is
we are meant to do?

All questions
are worthy of answers,
or for what reason
would we have to wonder,
we have to question.

In the finale
there could wellness be,
the inauguration of the end
of what we started out to do
in the very beginning.

Senior Moments

Gray cells synapsing
disappearing into the ozone

while I'm looking forever
for what's right in front of me

aging at the speed of light
is the ungluing of the universe

as I contemplate
the oneness of the world

a mindful exercise of being
in the moment

going beyond an ephemeral thought,
a shortness of breath,

and becoming reality
as I perceive it;

a cocktail of awe and wonder
with an olive of doubt.

Terminal Prognosis

A simple thank you
to the universe would do,
fine tuning the vibrations,
woven into braids of kindness
and care

From the shadows of a lung
a dark whole capable
of consuming the body
immerses the mind
in a fertile egoic winter
of motives, emotions,
I, me, and mine
taking center stage,
with time evaporating
in a terminal prognosis

Unless inevitability
can be overcome
life moves on
in prayer and promise

always grateful
for blessings in disguise

Old Habits

       humptydumptytumbled
ignominiously off the curb
and as habit would have it

      when his yoke broke
all that remained
a broken shell of himself

the story told over and over again
      as he was wont to do

an habitual circumstance
of letting and not letting go

old habits
      by their very nature
should always be a thing of the past

neither good nor bad
they either consciously succumb
          to the present

or subconsciously aid in one's demise

Re-Visiting Old Poems

memories of lovers
        forbidden smiles

old promises
        sitting in dust

patiently waiting on spring
        soon to be heard from

leaving the door open
        to the universe,

occasionally
        new friends

wander in and sit down
        beside you—

some   a few maybe,

        stay

What I see is only wallpaper

Faded favors I hold dear
artifacts to touch belonging
to the heart's content,
these are the soul possessions
I gather around me.

In rooms I have passed through
they are flocked patterns
on old stained surfaces,
the glue that held the moment together
dried and peeled, like memories
as unsustainable as the world I live in.

Old hangs on
as if it owned by a test of time,
each generation of paint
resurfacing walls
built only to stave off
the dogs of youth.

To hold on to insoluble control
of bric-a-brac, Machiavellian virtu,
the power of wrapping the world
in cellophane and dust—

Only to leave it all behind
        with a little flair
for the collective mind of greed;
for another horder of pretty things
to pass on by and tell the world
they can turn rocks into sand.

From where I stand,
for the space I know occupy
wallpaper is the perfect décor
yellowed from time, water stained,
weathered, yet defiantly attractive
on an unsustainable wall.

Stanislavsky's Superannuated Actors

The proscenium curtains open ante meridiem,
as the Mujer Gorda chimes, from time to time,
any number of miscues from the campanario.

The morning clarion on a motocicleta
rattles and rumbles on the cobblestones
delivering hot tortillas to the neighborhood,
never failing to miss his entrance when
huevos rancheros are planned for desayuno.

A grizzled actor scales a mountain of monologue
center stage, a run on off-off-Broadway, invariably
thanking
the audience for showing up.

The curtain closes only when the technician
turns off the spotlight on an empty house.

Post production a superannuated thespian
bidding time functioning on a prescript
of recall, refinement, while blocking blindly
with automatic choreographed steps, triggered
cues dependent on the memory of past acts.

Thankfully the body has a mind of its own
and Mime, the mummer Cat, with her tail in the air
critiques anything out of place.

Taking curtain-call in Mexico
to the applause of claques,
the grande drape closes
on another day of avoiding a recital
of fluffs, miscues, missteps, and muffs,
in an attempt to exit stage left,
methodically, while pantomiming
patience under a Ghost Light.

You Have Everywhere to Go

I have everywhere to go
and nowhere to get to,
other than where I am,
for reasons, not my own.

This senescence is never what I expected,
time a diminishing number of cells
doubling, in the immediate,
only potentially treatable.

Life it seems is what I wake up with.
All of a sudden it is today.

Sure, I have a few aches and pains,
daily my body expands and flattens,
my feet grow wider as I shrink.

Not going gently into night
bits and pieces fall apart
are manufactured
and left overnight on the nightstand.

It seems every morning the fractals
of my flesh have become more pronounced.
Bumps and blemishes appear and disappear,
mold, bacteria, and wrinkles
replacing the nip and tuck
of a body, once not in need of repair.

However, for reasons not my own,
a renewed presence continues
and everymorn is wonder
waiting for me to recognize.

I am here, having journeyed a lifetime
to get to where I have a need
to step out of the picture,
and elevate the consciousness of illusion
in an endeavor to know myself.

So It Is

So it is that old is
as old does
nurtured on the past.

Imagine everything
perceived as nothing
other than
a decaying dream.

Aging in an only lifetime,
the willow then
would last forever,
rebirthing in the soil
of content, birds would
sleep with the elephants,
aging would becomes a
thing of the past,
a shadow creeping
slowly up from behind.

Fragile is
as fragile does
tempered in the mold
cast before there ever was.

Bent and shaped by the wind
all remains
the same as always.

Some age like the oak
others like the weed,
all have work to do
all feed the soul
of the gardener
who plants the seed
and waits for
someone who knows
there is nothing to forgive.

so it is
through thick and thin
we learn to walk
we learn to swim
to crawl
from beneath the waves
time and time again

to say hello,
goodbye,
and in-between
a subtle sigh

The When & Where of It

When did the garden become a parking lot where after
a lifetime of reaching up to the heavens, the power of
gravity brought everything that rises toward the light
down to where it all began, to an empty lot devoid of
care where growing seasons suffered existence? Down
to a solitary bud demanding attention, its stem,
a climber on a beam of sunshine.

Given nothing of today and tomorrow by the Gardner,
reaching out to the light, seeking a place to be, the bud
began tinkering with the passage of time, ticking off
seconds, working on a to-do-list with the eventuality of
wrapping a life in daylight and darkness subject to the
whims of weather.

Nurtured in the genre handed down by the librarian of
circumstances, sometimes life is like reading a good
book, turning over a new leaf, one page at a time,
surrendering to the imagination, the luxury of being
human. So much of life is already written down,
previous chapters stored away in a memory box to be
dusted off on occasion with a curios thought.

Even if never nurturing a garden of words, it all
comes down to the end of a story, leaving only
the residue of when and where. No denouement
needed if a life well lived is one for the books.

When it comes to the finale, the last laugh, the inch
before the finish line, what lay in the fallow is fodder
for the forgotten, a primer for a fool's reward,
where the difference between the last hurrah, and
the silence of what could have been, is an if only.

*In the end, a romantic ballade to dance
to the music of one another.*

Making The Most Of The Twilight Years

Birthdays are more than just
a yearly trip down memory lane
they are a thankful reminder
you have lived long enough to celebrate.

Relationships don't just happen,
it takes what seems forever
to find the driftwood
that makes for a work of art
in the heart and mind of a drifter.

A dreamer means inventing colors,
bird-dogging rainbows,
being cocksure wishes come true
when you blow out the candles.

The yearly fête should be made
of the same ingredients
as the aroma of afterlove,
or that of a kitchen perfumed
with preparation for a feast for two,
to share in their twilight years.

Since We Talked Of Growing Old Together

I am slowly learning
to take a swift look at the past
& a sweet look at the future

when I hold autumn
against my senses

when the air hangs
with the aroma of fresh linen

when all the roses
are wearing raindrops

I don't suppose it matters
that it has only been forever

since we talked
        of growing old together

Dawn Breaks Across the Stillness of the Night

When dawn breaks across the stillness of the night,
and daylight filters through dreams of all we have
pleasured and pained.

We are there for each other boundlessly wrapped in
arms and legs, anchored to the soft and wonderful,
a wedded link to the possibility of all that is beautiful
in a relationship where someone listens, and cares.

Mornings are made for us. Our days open in a dance
of warmth and loving, one with the passage of light,
no shadows in and out of our hours together and apart.

Grumps, frumps and frailties of aging, churning out
the chapters of lives lived, melt beneath the covers drift
away with the passing moments of each and every day.

We have the pleasure of our company and the comfort
of knowing in our heart and soul we are fearlessly
where we want to be.

Yesterdays sauntered aimlessly and lulled about
heaven casting no shadow, leaving seldom behind.
Now it' is all in a day's grace this loving space we
are in, walking giftedly beside each other, no less
favored then before, but lighter footsteps and fewer
doors, with a companion to love, trust and adore.

As we journey now, on the evening of our lives
toward a sunset of the visible light, more spring
than fall, more time trailing behind us than to be
laid down, the life we share is not the beginning,
for we have always known each other, nor will it
be the end for we will always be together, forever
time and time again

The Ways You Walk Beside Me

These are the ways we walk together. Forgotten fears,
footsteps behind us dissipating in the laughter of our
growing old together, capable of having too much fun

As a friend in the garden we long since planted with
the soil of our spirit and desire, you enrich my union
with the earth, your water nourishes the very root of
my being me.

You look upon me without judgment, and when
momentarily I lose sight of who I am, I turn to my
friend and your light is always in the window, the way
to your heart always open. It is you I come to when I
want to be alone and need to be held.

As partners, palm-to-palm fingers entwined in wonder
at the world around us, venturing in unknown surprise
in a no fault relationship, trusting we are there f
or each other.

We talk to one another, I am in awe of your wisdom.
We share our space, and I am saturated with your
nearness. Side by side in cadence, indivisible in the
light, leaving one set of footprints in the silt and sands
of our memories.

As your lover, unblushingly undressed before the
mistress of my passions, you lovingly invite my touch,
my humbled hands conduct a symphony of joy.

You welcome the heat of my desire, my body
enters sacred ground finding, fulfillment in your
fantasies. My love lies down to sleep beside me.
I wil be be forever courting you in delight.

The companion of my dreams, your soft hands
laying beside my head holding the night together.
 I close my eyes knowing when I wake you will
be there beside me ,waiting as the dawn waits for
daylight. You say my name, "Good Morning,"
and I am at peace with myself.

As my spouse there is no bond between us. No
neediness or wantfullness, only loving the warm
comfort in a winter's darkness of our flesh folding
over one another.

A husband needing to come home to only you
to catch the moonlight as it lays shadows across your
body, wanting always to breathe you in.

Anniversary Gifts

Paper was an invitation pinned
to my bulletin board, an invitation
to a lifetime imagined, yet unimaginable,
when the undertow once ruled the shore.

When the waves receded, they left a dance
of footprints in the sand. Under a calico
sky of inhibitions and distrust were wet
bathing suits were discarded on the beach.

Tethered to the softest moment, fragility
dressed in lambskin *leather,* nothing could
break the bond, for the past was left behind.

Another year wrapped in *silk and linen*
for coming together under the gazebo.
Holding on and letting go, union of mind
where cats mellowed on the foot of the bed.

Wood came in driftwood, hope chests,
birch bark, weathering storms, as smooth
as an August evening. Time together polished
with a soft cloth, a path carved out of mahogany.

Limbs intertwined dancing in the wind. *Dark
Chocolate*. Sweet taste of afterlove. In a *crystal*
orb on a glass table. Candy for the soul.

If it's meant to be, the stitches hold. The universe
returns favor and momentarily pauses to let
wounds and words heal. Healing stimulates change,
years pass, cast in *bronze,* promises are upheld,

We were meant to be the ones on the shore
gathering stones and shells, Never letting go,
coupling at the hip where fantasy flatters reality.

All that is wished for once pinned to a treasure map,
a dream in the making for being here, coexisting
with the hibiscus, the hummingbird, sunlight & shade,
hand in hand fashioned in *silver, steel, jade, lace.*

Something about aging, that wants to
hold hands with someone.

HELLO OUT THERE!

sometimes
I wish I could just call
        and say hello

say how time has squandered
what could have been
        time well spent

knowing more about you,
filling in the gaps between
        then and now.

living long,
in the scheme of things,
does not always bring clarity

carries with it a head full
of what if's, a belly full
of if only questions
        unasked, unanswered.

if I had only known,
I would have listened, instead
of being preoccupied with living

Esto lo Se

This you know
is where the water springs forth

where we bathe
in the luxury of life
and slip beneath the surface
barely a ripple
for having been here
some of us hang in here
like energizer bunnies
daring the universe to let go

some miss the morning
wake up call
and leave a hole
in the evening sky
where once a star shone brightly

others just tired of it all
we send on ceramic vessels
to where good memories
come to rest
in the underwater shrines
of Lake Chapala

This you know is where
we all come to say goodbye

Soft Landings

I take myself with me
wherever I go dust settles

It has all come together aquí–
the shoreline of my youth

The mountains in my dreamtime,
the myth of vulnerability exposed
to sunlight and color,

After the rain, after putting together,
Humpty and climbing down off the fence

my daemon and I,
sharing a frosted margarita
over the hero's homecoming

Abaft Aggrandizement

A lasting a-literat-ion lays an apotheosis
on life, with the human habit of hanging

around in the heavens, on mountain tops
and hallowed grounds, instead of saying

enough already content with a peaceful
ephemeral life instead of wanting to be,

etched on endemic edifices, pedestals,
plaques, and memorialized in praying,

all in keeping with the old age adage
love can linger after the lights go out.

Comes a Time

Comes a time, comes a time for dying when the shadow walks away. Up until it dawned on me in an evening of sunsets, it wasn't anything I paid much attention to. Lacking an extended family to speak of, in half a century anyone who passed left me out of the equation. Everyone in my life came and went like two trains going in the opposite direction, a blur of faces in the windows.

I remember my first coffin. In grade 6 the nuns marched us out of class and across the street to Dwyer Funeral Home to say a meek little benediction over the body of someone they told us was important. To this day I cannot lie on my back with my hands folded over my chest. As an adult I avoided funerals as an end of life ceremony and preferred to remember the good things about the person I had known, that way they never really died on me.

My mother at 87 was the first personal close encounter with the reality that there really was the possibility I would end up in the proverbial dustbin. No open coffin though, cremation without ceremony was her option—she was heading straight for heaven. That was a lifetime ago. Since then aging has played games with the face in the mirror. And although I'm not particularly thrilled about having to end the journey I'm on, in the end the choice will be a foregone conclusion.

I do know that I have come full circle. In youth when everyday was sunrise and life engrossed all my senses, dying was a destiny I gave no thought to, and now having discarded time as irrelevant, reveling in the life that surrounds me, relegates death to just a likely possibility when the music stops playing. I can now reflect on the knowledge that dying is a part of living. Never so clear to me now that I live in a small

Mexican village where it is an accepted part of daily life. For the first time I have been able to visit my neighbors coffin and remember him as he was and always will be in the hearts of those who passed his way. The familia celebración of el Abuelo brought tears to my eyes, not only for the sadness of those left behind, but for all the celebrations I missed thinking death was not something I cared to pay mind to.

No matter how long it takes there is an ending to everything. Is it possible that what I was after, after all, was an expression of self, and that's all I will leave behind. In the finale there could wellness be, the inauguration of the end of what I started out to do in the very beginning. I still cannot lie back with my hands folded over my chest, not for fear of dying, but because I want to reach out and hold on to everything.

A Coming of Age

As a certifiable Septuagenarian I now, on occasion think about aging and growing old. I suppose it comes with the body politic. Never have liked the word "old" unless, as Francis Bacon remarked it appears to be best in four things; old wood best to burn, old wine to drink, old friends to trust, and old authors to read.

A 2009 Pew Research study indicated that the average respondent believed old age begins in the mid-sixties, and older as opposed to younger believed old age started at a much later point. That's a no brainer. In a Daily Mail article, according to young Brits, old age starts at 52. I'll have none of it. I knew someday if the good lord willing I might reach the seventh age of man described by Jacque in William Shakespeare's *As You Like It*; as second childishness and mere oblivion, sans teeth, sans eyes, sans taste, sans everything…and all that didn't sound too appealing to me.

Living in the Berkshires of Western Massachusetts old was in; New Yorkers and Bostonians fought over decrepit chairs and 3 legged tables once buried in the dust of damp and moldy barns, on sale as priceless antiques of the not so ancient pilgrims. Malcolm Cowley in his book of personal essays, *The View from Eighty* he quotes an octogenarian friend "They tell you that you lose your mind when you grow older, but what they don't tell you is that you won't miss if very much."

The word "old" needs a little help standing on its own, and it has nothing to do with canes and walkers, it's the tags that follows it around like an old dog: "old bag," "old fogey," and "old timer." I can relate to defining old as of former times, like "days of old," having been aged for a comparatively long time, as in old brandy. My commanding officer in the Air

Force was the "old man," and that was acceptable. Unacceptable would be the terminology dating back to 1775 for wife or mother as the "old lady". That might have worked for the founding fathers but politically incorrect today. Mi Esposa occasionally has to remind me "you're getting old honey," but that's usually when certain parts of my anatomy won't take no for an answer.

The word aging on the other hand is the process of becoming older. In the narrow sense, the term refers to biological aging of human beings, and other living creatures. Gabriel García Márquez, in *Memories of My Melancholy Whores* writes "Age isn't how old you are but how old you feel."

Lewis Thomas writes in his book of essays *The Fragile Species*: "It is possible to say all sorts of good things about aging when you are talking about aging free of meddling diseases. It is an absolutely unique stage of human life—the only stage in which one has both the freedom and the world's blessing to look back and contemplate what has happened during one's lifetime instead of pressing forward to new high deeds."

Here's the rub, things can and do go south in the process of aging: one thing after another goes wrong, and the cumulative impact of these failures is the image of aging. However, normal aging is not a disease at all, but a stage of living that cannot be averted or bypassed except in one way, nicely summed up by Maurice Chevalier; "Old age isn't so bad when you consider the alternative. Nevertheless many regard aging as a slow death with everything going wrong. Florida Pier Scott-Maxwell, a playwright, author and psychologist, nearing her nineties wrote "When a new disability arrives, I look about me to see if death has come, and I call quietly, 'Death, is that you? Are you there?' and so far the disability has answered, 'Don't be silly. It's me."

When I finally did come to the awareness I was aging somewhat, I was encouraged by the latest discoveries in cell biology—my body, with a few exceptions has a makeover every 10 years or so with old cells discarded and new ones generated, the pace depending on the workload. Why I don't act my physical age is because there are some ornery cells hanging in there from birth to death. My brain has mind of its own and doesn't generate new neurons except in mediating the sense of smell, and where I remember faces and places. I'm not there yet, but I guess someday I could be referred to as an old fart.

Doris Lessing wrapped it all up for me when she said, "The great secret that all old people share is that you really haven't changed in seventy or eighty years. Your body changes, but you don't change at all. And that, of course, causes great confusion." I want to think I've aged more like a gem of polished driftwood washed up on a white sandy shore rather than a gnarly old oak tree all bark, no bite.

Senescent Choices

Life it seems is what I wake up with. All of a sudden it is today. Sure, I have a few aches and pains. Daily my body expands and flattens, my feet grow wider as I shrink. Not going gently into night bits and pieces fall apart, are manufactured and left overnight on my nightstand.

I am here, having journeyed a lifetime to get to where I have a need to step out of the picture, and elevate the consciousness of illusion in an endeavor to know myself. We don't travel on an unmarked road, however, it is possible to miss the milestones and signs along the way that provide choices.

Sometimes we need to recollect what just happened along the route in order to make sense of it all. Sometimes oncoming decisions need to be made immediately without the opportunity to reflect, and if we don't pay attention, the road may just come to a dead end having missed our cutoff. That's where choice comes in. Cancer was a sign that said time to turn here.

A sexagenarian friend of mine is financially able to retire comfortably, but remains dedicated to pursuing a line of work he says all his previous working life has led him to. After an expensive divorce, a bout with cancer and lingering aftermath, an early golden handshake, and a gift card from the government for officially being old, you'd think it would be time to stop expanding in the universal scheme of things, whoadown, slow down, leave behind the rebound, spend time staying healthy doing the daily comealong, and not much more. Anything *but* back to work. Yet. Who knows where that road may lead?

I'm not saying that it's ever time to stop. If you don't use it, you know, it wears down from lack of friction with life, and rusts. Neuroscience research shows the brain's biological growth reaches full maturity around age 25. If it did keep growing no one would be able to wear those ubiquitous baseball caps

Continuous higher learning and occupational attainment, on the other hand changes the brain and every experience brings on cognitive growth. Decision making, planning, relationships, the part of the brain that makes us human just keeps chucking along when we use it, for better or worse.

H.L. Mencken's observation that the older he grew, the more he distrusted the familiar doctrine that age brings wisdom probably has some merit based on some of the curmudgeons I know. Older brains chock full of expert erudition relevant to a pursuit or passion when utilized for solving problems and coming up with solutions slows the mental aging process.

So who's to say which is the better choice, keeping the pedal to the metal on the road you're on, or taking the next turn to follow your dreams? No matter how long it takes there is an ending to everything. Is it possible that what we are after, after all, is an expression of self, and in that an understanding of what it is we are meant to do?

All choices are worthy of consideration, or for what reason would we have to wonder, we have to question. I made the choice to follow my dream and take the exit heading for a quiet (sometimes) small village on the shore of Lake Chapala, Mexico and have no regrets. As John Barrymore put it: man is not old until regrets take the place of dreams."

PEWS

Notwithstanding the pickling and pruning of the average genarian the most widely seen cognitive change associated with aging is that of the Procedural, Episodic, Working, and Semantic memory. The functioning or lack of is uniquely personal and can be of some concern. Personally this memory/recall thing doesn't really bother me until I think about it. If you live long enough all the closets in the upper house become cluttered with stuff you only go looking for when something or someone plants a seed, otherwise out of sight, out of mind.

I know I'm not alone when I leave my mind behind—climbing the stairs, entering a room going after something that, just an interminable second ago, was the most important priority, focus, quest on my agenda, only to return to the origin of the thought to re-enact what it might have been that I was after.

Perhaps it's not that my motor skills are any less vibrant than when I was younger—I still remember how to ride a bike, it just that I'm not all that interested anymore in pedaling about, and I still could walk, talk and chew gum at the same time if it weren't for my dentures. When it comes to how to do stuff I may have forgotten a few things, but now I know how to find it on YouTube or Wikihow.com.

Early grade school left me with just one off the top of my head episodic memory: the little old lady teaching grade 5 periodically zoning out and starting to take her clothes off in the front of the class, and someone always running to get a nun. Those mental tags about where, when and how information is picked up don't sit out there on a garage sale table waiting to be plucked, they have to be searched for, and the search gets a little more interesting with the ageing process.

Working at trying to manipulate the present is like trying to altering the past, and processing information is more work than the curmudgeon in me generally wants to deal with. Irritability comes on when decision making demands a perceived unreasonableness. I know if I pay attention I just might learn a thing or two, and if I'm lucky it will stick.

Seemingly patience has become my patron saint of forgetfulness. It allows me to abdicate responsibility in the land-of-forget-me-nots where greycells become the dandruff of should haves and oops, maybe, if only I had remembered what I ... Sometimes it's just lazy mind. With the esposa a walking rolodex, I don't really have to dig deep in the recesses of the skull for the names of people that I meet, and when searching for the meaning of things, Google has usurped my semantic memory, transferring recall from my cerebral cortex to my fingertips.

Do we really need to remember every name, place, event, taste, smell, song etc., why not take every new encounter as a surprise—a fresh face, a familiar but exotic smell, a subtle and refreshing taste, an exquisite moment, the feeling brought on by sound of the Moonlight Sonata. I have learned, and keep reminding myself, I need only to be the keeper of the world around me to relive the memory of all that I have known and cared for. I need to be joyful of memory and open to what comes along when it does, and when it does I'll be seated in the first pew, knowing it will unfold in its own time at the altar of love.

In-Between Before and After

I was floundering on, as usual, until she gave my soul a slap—well deserved at that. I dug myself out of the fiction of life and devoured the books on enlightenment she gave me to read. She wondered if I had the will power to see the light. It was all candlelight at first. Then slowly, over time, my mind's eye adjusted to the sunlight that entered my life.

Maybe it helped, maybe it didn't. I hit bottom and bounced back. I got a job with insurance. If that wasn't bait enough to entice her to give it another go— I finally had a home for her to come back to. I was still dubious about whether angels actually existed, at least in my dimension. Until that is, I decided to quit smoking. I did it the hard way—lung cancer. And those new age guru quantum mystic holistic health specialists she turned me on to—maybe they helped, maybe they didn't, but at least I'm not now working on re-incarnation therapy.

She was a reluctant angel, but she saved my life. Because of her I learned to listen. What baffles the body at times undermines the spirit. Yet the body-mind intention is ever clear. The essence of some sensibility so out of place, so foreign in a private space—was there—and wanted me to be aware. I had come to understand that what is received by one cell, entering the vast emptiness, is complete in every sense. Nothing enters the body and is not heard, and I heard the cancer deep in the dark recesses of my lung.

Everybody knows about the hole in the bucket. It's where reality, the visible world on the other side of the plate glass window of your mind, slowly leaks into the emptiness of time and space. Until one day you find you have arrived in the here and now, and the bucket's empty.

How was it that the illusion of happiness, the

lingering smell of sweat and damp sheets, the cocoon of comfort wrapped around my brain, could, in the course of a conversation, over a cup of coffee, or sitting on the edge of the bed, turn into an aloneness, without substance, an accumulation of a lifetime of togetherness with nothing to hold onto. Waking to nobodies home anymore means meant I was left with my own rewards.

She had told me it was never complicated—if you can't cook, stay out of the kitchen. If you don't love yourself, leave romance well enough alone. I had put her emails in a folder in my memory box along with the record album of the music we loved—it had a groove in it where the heartache began.

Then & Now

It is approaching summer and a dead leaf lies in the wet grass visibly shaking in the wind, as if it had a season of splendor ahead of it to foliage in the stifling green of the Berkshires. Each day in New England trembles with the excitement of not knowing which way the wind blows, cold and damp or hot and humid. Here mold grows between the teeth of timber, and under the fingernails of anything that scratches above the surface of the firmament. I am here for whatever reason the universe is nudging me towards eternity, and I am thankful for the Innkeepers courtesy. Everything I do lends itself to everything I need to do, subconsciously, or in my face, to get to where I have always been moving towards.

Some days are better than others. This is not a frivolous axiom but a fact of passing through. If one travels down memory lane, those long stretches of highway, were nothing passes but the lines between oncoming trials and tribulations, and all of that that lingers momentarily in the rear view mirror; what should remain is those short breaths of life coming from a whisper of thank you. There is no need to shout or exclaim, for anything a decibel above silence is all that is needed to revel in the beauty of the moment.

Mi esposa waits on my journey south. When togetherness is but a week away, after a long journey through a winter apart, separation brings a sadness that needs only a sweet hello, a smile, an eye to eye understanding that longing is no longer a part of communication.

Behind me a blur of activity, dissolution and expectation sliding into a distant memory, the cork swollen and dry, never again needing to fit, for the bottle well received is graciously empty. Nothing left for the gods. The names of faces and places never forgotten, like the last drabs of winter's snow wait on the curb ready to fall into the gutter and disappear down the drain. Three thousand miles later, the street sweepers brush away the remnants of a winter's memory while a golden butterfly dances on the light of a brilliant bougainvillea.

Days now have names like Lunes, Viernes, Sabado and Domingo, and come and go at their own pace, in this place, now called home. A dominion of diamonds and dust where wealth buys you a view and more rooms then you'll ever need to live in; and outside the life of this place where the chickens leave eggs on your doorstep, is waiting on your embrace.

When the connection between then and now times out, it doesn't really matter. You're mind refocuses on the immediate, dogs talk to one another and their barks echo across the mountains with the boom booms. There is a constant cluck and trill nullifying chatter, implanting the sheen of after rain on the blossoms of a peaceful mind. Dawn has shifted from the alarming dark entrance into day's hustle—the 5 a.m. lurch into insanity; to a subtle awareness, casually around 8 or 9; the gentle scraping at the bedroom door suggesting the cats want breakfast, roosters rolling their r's wafting in chorus from the village below, a mist of light washing the dust from your eyes, an appreciation that life has for the moment in eternity, settled here on the shores of Lake Chapala.

La Vista

If there is one thing aging expats have in common its having traveled far and wide, and one of the things we might have noticed is the human penchant for seeking the high ground. It is the domain of the wealthy and the spiritual, the adventurous and the driven, it is home for castles and monasteries and for the life of us we dig our way out of holes, climb ladders of success, reach for diamonds in the sky.

Like the Jefferson's "Moving on up" from the basement apartment to the penthouse is what most, not all, seem to strive for. If you're on top of the world, you're haute-monde, carriage trade, opulent, majestic, gated, upper crust sitting pretty with an exquisite view of the digs, shanties, hovels and the lower class. It's all in the words of course, but the reality is some words are dressed in linen, some in burlap, some are birds perched on the topmost tip of a tree, others potted plants on a window sill thirsting for a patch of sky. Like Flannery O'Connor's Everything That Rises Must Converge, we all want the same things out of life—to rise above the darkness and share the light.

Light, like a rodent scavenging the recesses of darkened rooms, seldom reaches the impoverished eye, where portals for air called windows, open to shadows. As far as one can see in the tenements of light, a mirror image of distance beyond reach. No wonder we seek the highest landing, for to see as far as one can see, through a wall of glass, from where only clouds and inner sanctums of the mind effects the quality of light, is where butterflies stay warm and we're all meant to be.

My neighbor, just a measure below me, has an unobstructed view of Lake Chapala and a sierra of mountain on the southern shore. My view, although not as expansive—cluttered with Bougainvillea and palm trees—is equally rewarding to the senses. There the commonality becomes a metaphor for the beauty of the moment. He sits under a weather beaten plastic tarp, I sit on a shaded deck, both of us knowing height, for the most part, is a barrier between owning the heavens and hugging the earth.

There are mountains in the sky that no one can climb, rooted to this planet as we are. There are such things unheard of, out of grasp, hidden still to the yet unborn, privy only to another lifetime, yet, like a silhouetted mistress, taunting, inviting one into the realm of unimaginable secrets, the sense of being demands attention to the possibilities, each breath taking in all the dreams and wishes, all the fears and failures of those who have tried to shed the skin of mortality and reach a higher plane.

Late in life I am able to see farther than I have ever been able to, not for a distance diminished by the light in my eyes, but by the knowing beyond the wall of the visible, the endless beauty of creation is all in my imagination, it is all in the wonder of what, in the moment of perception, for the life of me, I experience.

There are mountains of cloud billowing in the sky that beckon us, to climb out of the dark matter of our minds, scale the imagination, leaving doubt behind, to finally achieve, in the heights of mystical possibility, a glimpse of understanding.

The Pleasure of Her Company

If life is but a borrowing of bones, we cannot speak for one another when it comes to calling a place home. When we stumble or slide into a space that makes living in the moment satisfying to the soul, we can share what we discover about ourselves, for you take yourself with you wherever you go and dust settles.

Dawn lay in bed this morning as if not wanting to get up, the earth turning on a breeze, still *lago*, still *montañas*. As the Turquoise Prince, the Aztec sun and war god, yawns awake, I too linger under the covers until *el gallo* screeches the sound of turning the key while the motor is on, and my neighbor Maria, outside her *choza*, starts up her washing machine. I lay dormant until the automatic carafe kicks in and the seductive aroma of Veracruz Organic lures me to my terrace.

It has all come together *aquí*—the shoreline of my youth, the mountains in my dreamtime, the myth of vulnerability exposed to sunlight and color.

I have the pleasure and the comfort of knowing in my heart and soul mi esposa and I are where we want to be. Yesterdays sauntered aimlessly and lulled about heaven, casting no shadow, now it's all in a day's grace this loving space we are in, walking beside each other no less favored than before but lighter footsteps and fewer doors with a companion to love, trust and adore. As we journey now in the evening of our lives towards a sunset of the visible light, more spring than fall, more time trailing behind us than to be laid down, the life we share is not the beginning, it is a forevermore.

At first we danced the *mazurka*. We were younger then, our steps in tune to the beat of our hearts, *waltzing* in and out of each year, always chasing rainbows in a whimsy *fantasia*. Now that life is a *polonaise*, a slow march on the ivories, we look forward to an evening *nocturne*, and on this one of many days in the village of Ajijic, where the water springs forth, a romantic *ballade* to dance to the music of one another.

ABOUT THE AUTHOR

Born in the US and raised in Canada John now resides in the tranquil village of Ajijic in Jalisco, Mexico, where he shares his life with his wife, Candis, and a cherished clowder of furry companions.

John Thomas Dodds has self-published a collection of 15 volumes, of poetry on prominent online platforms. His repertoire includes two enchanting children's books composed in verse, *A Sneaky Twitch of an Itch* and *The Journey Home.* Under the pen name J.T. Dodds, he has crafted five novels: a trilogy *To Each Their Own Goodbye*, consisting of Book 1: *Anywhere Except Yesterday*, "Book 2: *A Long Way From Nowhere*, and Book 3: *When Tomorrow Is Never Enough,* and two standalone novel titled *If You Are Born To Be A Tamale,* and *Wanting To Breathe Her In.*